The Author's Magic Key

How to Stay on Track and Keep the Faith

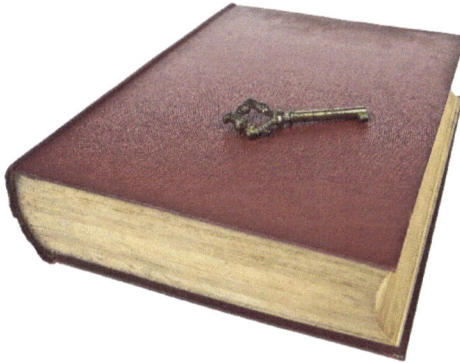

Kim Staflund

The Author's Magic Key
How to Stay on Track and Keep the Faith

From the author who brought us

*How to Publish a Book in the East
That You Can Sell in the West* in which
"The author has used the simplest words which can be
read and understood by everyone. The stepwise
information makes this book seamless and interesting."
by Sheetal Maurya, Godse (Halo of Books)

and

How to Publish a Bestselling Book wherein
"...Staflund gives good advice and it's remarkably far-
reaching, considering that it covers several countries ...
[A]n enlightening, helpful book which gives you an
excellent introduction to the business of publishing."
by The Bookbag

Kim Staflund
Polished Publishing Group (PPG)

The Author's Holy Trinity of Profit (Book Three)

The Author's Magic Key: How to Stay on Track and Keep the Faith
Ebook ISBN: 978-1-988971-38-4
Paperback ISBN: 978-1-988971-39-1
© 2019 by Kim Staflund

🍁PolishedPublishingGroup

Due to the dynamic nature of the Internet, any website addresses mentioned within this book might have been changed or discontinued since its publication.

For creators:

"Books are uniquely portable magic."
~Stephen King

The Author's Holy Trinity of Profit Trilogy

Action
*The Author's Money Tree: How to Grow a
Bountiful Readership Organically*

Thought
*The Author's Gold Rush: How to Harvest a
Bountiful Crop Repeatedly*

Faith
*The Author's Magic Key: How to Stay on Track and
Keep the Faith*

TABLE OF CONTENTS

INTRODUCTION

Just as it takes three full seasons to reap the *true* rewards of The Author's Money Tree, there are three necessary components to achieving your goals. Action. Thought. Faith. The final book in this trilogy, *The Author's Magic Key*, focuses on helping you develop a strong faith in yourself.

The Magic Key to Faith

To see this plan through to fruition, you'll need to have complete confidence and trust in what you're doing. You'll need to hold true to your goals even on those days when your progress seems slower than you'd like.

One of the best ways to develop faith is to read the stories of others who have succeeded before you. This book is filled with many of the sources I often turn to for inspiration. Some of these people are authors. Others are business owners, actors, or athletes. They all have one thing in common: a strong, unwavering faith in their own abilities that was developed over time.

The Magic Key to Focus

They also have a laser focus on reaching their desired goals, whatever those goals may be. They visualize their desired result daily before taking action. And they train their brains with the use of affirmations, as recommended by Napoleon Hill:

> The method by which one develops *faith*, where it does not already exist, is extremely difficult to describe. Almost as difficult, in fact, as it would be to describe the color of red to a blind man. Faith is a state of mind that you may develop at will …

Making repeated affirmations to your subconscious mind is the only known method of developing the emotion of faith voluntarily. (Hill, 1937)

This book is filled with many teachers who can help you achieve your goals under any circumstance. Even if you don't have any "cheerleaders" around you.

The Magic Key to Endurance

Let's face it, some days are easier than others when it comes to sticking to any goal. We all have our moments of doubt. Sometimes, it would be easier to quit.

It doesn't matter who you are, you're going to have setbacks. It's at those times when you'll need a little boost to help you get back on track. In this book, I've included the inspirational stories of several people who have succeeded before you. But I don't want you to see their successes alone; in fact, I want you to see their failures. Because I want you to see how they got back up again—how they endured through difficult times—so you know you can do it, too.

Whenever you're struggling along your journey as an author, I hope you'll pick up this book and read it. Remind yourself why you're doing what you're doing. Use these words to restore your faith and move forward.

IT ALL STARTS WITH A CLEAR VISION

This book is not only for all the authors out there who have already published and want guidance on how to sell more books. It's for those of you who continue to procrastinate on taking that next step toward publishing. What you're lacking is a clear vision of what's coming ahead. I'll show you how to create one for yourself so you can move forward with faith.

I get asked this question a lot: Will you read and critique my manuscript for me? Possibly. But not for free. Because this is an editing service—a paid service—that must be completed by a professional editor.

I find that many people request this even after they've already had two or three friends or colleagues read and critique a manuscript for them. Those people gave it a rave review, and now they're looking for ... what? Another rave review? Or maybe a criticism—a way out?

I always ask these people, "And what will happen if *I* like the book? Or what if I don't like it? Then what? Will you bring it to someone else to read and critique? Or will you finally stop procrastinating, finish writing it, have it edited and designed, and publish it once and for all?"

The only critics who *truly* matter are your readers—your customers. And the only way you'll learn what they like and don't like is to publish it and read their reviews. You'll grow and learn from there if you keep yourself open to growing and learning.

Every author experiences criticism along the way. It's okay. I get five-star and three-star reviews, and even the occasional one-star review of my books online. After several years of doing this, I've grown a thicker skin and have learned that *I* have to love me and my books first—*I* have to support my vision first—and other people's approval (whether it comes or not) is extra; it doesn't make or break me anymore. Now, when someone gives me one star with an unflattering review attached to it, I simply thank them for taking the time to read and comment on my book; then I recommend another book that they may enjoy better. End of story. Move on. You'll learn to do the same over time.

Maybe, some of that comes with age. I love this stage in my life. Why? Because, in middle age, I've reached a place where I know some people like me, some don't, some people agree with me, some don't. And I can live with that. It's a peaceful place to be.

> "Some failure in life is inevitable. It is impossible to live without failing at something, unless you live so cautiously that you might as well not have lived at all—in which case, you fail by default."
> ~J. K. Rowling, 2008 Harvard Commencement Speech

In other words, you fail by default if you never publish your book. But you have a strong chance of success if you go through with it—publish it and then sell it by following the steps set out for you in this series. Just *do* it, already!

Throughout this final book in the series, I want to share some of my greatest sources of inspiration—people who have taught me to keep the faith when I was feeling down after a bad review or just plain frustrated that there were no reviews or sales at all. Every single one of these winners experienced failures, criticisms, and disappointments of their own along the way. But they kept the faith and kept working toward their respective goals.

Eventually, they won over their critics. Or, in the very least, they proved them wrong.

> "The greatest revenge is massive success."
> ~Tony Robbins

If you don't have a clear vision of where you want to go with your book business right now, that's okay. Don't push it. Read through this book series to get an idea of what's actually possible for you. Then ask for the specific plan that will bring you joy and success with your books. Send that prayer out into the cosmos and keep yourself open to receiving the answer. Have faith that it will come to you just as it did for the following people.

Her "Idea Moment" Came to Her Before the Actual Idea

You may have heard of Sara Blakely, the now-billionaire founder of Spanx. But are you aware of her humble beginnings and everything she went through to build her empire? I've researched this woman intently over the last few years, and her story is truly inspirational. She's one of the most accessible, down-to-earth, humorous, and likeable business leaders I've ever come across in my studies. Her story started with a simple vision as described in a CNN interview with Poppy Harlow (which is posted on YouTube for all to view for free).

Her "idea moment," as she calls it, happened *before* the actual idea for her business came to her. She was unhappy with her mundane job as a door-to-door fax machine salesperson, and she began to visualize a new life and career for herself. Her intention began simply as, "I want to invent something that I can sell to millions of people, and I want the product to make people feel good."

The invention, itself, came to her in a moment of frustration some time later. She was getting dressed for an evening out, and she couldn't find anything to wear underneath her white pants that would smooth out panty lines and hide cellulite. That's when she cut the feet out of her control-top pantyhose and put those on under her pants. This provided the "smooth canvass" she was after and helped her to look even more toned and slim. The problem was, the pantyhose rolled up her legs all night. So, she decided, then and there, that she would invent footless pantyhose to solve this issue for herself and all other women.

His Blueprint to Success Was Laid Out for Him in a Magazine Article

Whether you like Arnold Schwarzenegger's movies or agree with his political views, I think we can all agree he is a successful man—in more than one area of his life. In fact, he has conquered physical fitness, money, the movie business, *and* the political arena. But none of these roads were easy for him to travel.

Arnold came from very humble beginnings, born in a little village in Austria after World War II. He describes growing up in a country stricken by depression, alcoholism, famine, and poverty caused by Germany's defeat in that war. He always knew he wanted to get out of there; he wanted a better life for himself. But nothing about his surroundings provided any degree of hope for anything more.

During school one day, Arnold created his vision while watching a video about the successful United States of America with its tall skyscrapers, large freeways, and magnificent bridges. He fell in love with the idea of living in America and began to visualize one day living there himself. Of course, international travel was uncommon back then. Nobody had much money. So, he had no idea how he could possibly make this vision come true.

A few years later, he came across an article about Reg Park in a bodybuilding magazine titled "How Mr. Universe Became a Hercules Star." He read through it and realized this was his ticket to America: an award-winning bodybuilding career followed by a notable acting career. The whole "blue print" was laid out for him, right before his eyes. At 15 years old, Arnold became a bodybuilder with that vision clear in his mind. He worked out five or six hours per day, just as Reg had done, to progress toward his goal a little more each day.

This Man Dubbed His Calling "The Church of Freedom from Concern"

As a fellow Canadian, Jim Carrey has a special place in my heart. In one of the most inspirational speeches I've ever heard (which is posted on YouTube for all to listen to for free), he describes how the pain of his childhood became the catalyst for his own vision of success.

> "My father could have been a great comedian, but he didn't believe that that was possible for him, and so he made a conservative choice. Instead, he got a safe job as an accountant. And when I was 12 years old, he was let go from that safe job, and our family had to do whatever we could to survive. I learned many great lessons from my father, not the least of which was that you can fail at what you *don't* want. So, you might as well take a chance on doing what you love."
> ~Jim Carrey, 2014 Maharishi University of Management Commencement Address

Following his father's lay-off, Jim and his family lost their home and had to live in a van for a time. Worse yet, at age 15, he had to quit school and take a job as a janitor to help support his family. It was a traumatic time for him, to say the least.

Still, Jim could see the *positive* effect that his father's love and humour had on everyone around him—even in the most difficult of times. He saw, through his dad, a beautiful life purpose he could emulate himself. Back then, his decision to become a comedian was more about helping ease other peoples' pain—freeing them from concern—than becoming "rich and famous." Once he realized this life purpose, his vision became crystal clear to him; and he dubbed his new devotion (his "ministry") The Church of Freedom from Concern. That is how he decided he would serve the world in this lifetime. Isn't that beautiful? And look how far that vision has taken him.

She Just Didn't Want to Live *This* Way Anymore

Lisa Nichols inspires me! Because she's so real. She's so unapologetically *real*. You can pull up any number of YouTube videos of her speaking, or you can read her bestselling books, and you'll see exactly what I mean.

In the 1990s, Lisa Nichols was a single parent supporting herself and her son, Jelani, on government welfare. Her son's father had just gone to jail. One night, she experienced her version of "rock bottom" when she went to an automated teller to withdraw $20 so she could buy diapers for her son … but there were insufficient funds in the account. Lisa ended up having to wrap her baby boy in towels for two days because she couldn't afford to buy diapers. During one of these evenings, she put her hand on his stomach and promised him, "I will never be this broke or broken ever again."

Lisa's dream didn't start as a grand vision of becoming the multimillionaire public speaker and media personality she now is. It started simply as a firm decision that she wouldn't live *this* way anymore—always struggling to make ends meet. As someone who was raised in a rough part of South Central Los Angeles, she knew that *statistically* her son had a very high chance of joining a gang or ending up in prison like his father had. So, to transform their lives, she knew she would have to leave the area and seek out new influences and opportunities. That's when Lisa became an avid student of abundance and prosperity which eventually led her to becoming a teacher of abundance and prosperity for others through her company that she has aptly named Motivating the Masses.

This Woman Asked God to Give Her a Platform to Do Good

As early as four years old, Oprah Winfrey recalls standing on the back porch of her home and watching her grandmother boiling clothes because they didn't have a washing machine. Even at that early age, she told herself, "My life won't be like this. It will be better." Oprah knew she had a different calling, although that calling wasn't clear to her yet at that time.

Her vision became a little clearer years later, in her early twenties, when she was working in television. She longed to be an actress more than a news anchor or talk show host, but she was unwilling to give up a job she knew so many others wanted. So, Oprah decided she would have to be discovered somehow through her television appearances. And that's exactly how it happened for her.

One day, she read what she believed was the perfect role for her inside a book, and she began visualizing herself in that role.

> **7:49 location on video:** I truly believe that thoughts are the greatest vehicle to change, power, and success in the world. Everything begins with thoughts. … I thought up The Color Purple [film] for myself. I know this is going to sound strange to you. I read the book. I got so many copies of that book. I passed the book around to everybody I knew. If I was on the bus, I'd pass it out to people. And, when I heard that there was going to be a movie, I started talking it up for myself. I didn't know Quincy Jones or Steven Spielberg, or how on earth I would get in this movie. I'd never acted in my life. But I felt it so intensely that I had to be a part of that movie. I just, I really do believe that I created it for myself. (Winfrey)

Later, Oprah's vision became more profound than simply wanting to be an actress. She wanted to be able to change people's lives for the better, and she realized that television gave her the most incredible platform for that influence. Before every Oprah show, she did a mental meditation—a prayer—to ensure the correct message would get across to her millions of viewers. And the "correct message" she intended to get across through each show is that we're all responsible for our own lives, no matter what is going on around us. Even in tragedy, there is always an opportunity to triumph.

He Wanted to Help Other People Escape and Feel Inspired

For many of us, watching any of the Rocky movies serves as an instant and powerful source of motivation to get up off one's butt and *achieve*! Well, the life story of the man behind those movies is even more impactful. Sylvester Stallone's road to success is a real "rags to riches" story about what's truly possible if you stay focused on a goal, and he's one of my top sources of inspiration whenever I need a mental and emotional boost.

Like Oprah, Sylvester wanted to be in the movie business since he was very young. He wasn't interested in a television career—only movies. His compelling reason for this, which had him take some extreme risks that may make other people shutter, was that he saw movies as an opportunity to help other people escape and feel inspired. Just as his Rocky movies show people what they're truly capable of and how to overcome incredible odds, so does his own drive to get the first film in that series made.

My Own Vision Has Always Been About Travel and Freedom

I started Polished Publishing Group (PPG) as a "digital publishing company" in November 2009. In retrospect, I didn't fully understand *effective* digital publishing at that time. Nearly ten years later, I can confidently say I do, and the way I run my company has evolved as a result. That's usually how it happens for people. There will be twists and turns in the road as you navigate your way toward your vision. That's okay. Just keep your eye on the goal and trust that you'll get there eventually. Enjoy the journey and all its lessons along the way. I know *I* have.

From the start, my goal has always been to operate my business in a virtual office environment, untethered from any particular geographic location. I've seen myself leading by example with my own successful books while helping others to achieve success with theirs. In my mind's eye, I visualize attending book fairs, writing conferences, and author events all around the world—networking with my cherished industry peers (e.g., authors, publishers, booksellers, agents), and posting educational/inspirational success stories about them on my YouTube channel and podcast. As time goes on, I'd much rather work *with* people (help each other) than compete against anyone. I see this industry evolving into one where writers now have an honest opportunity to earn a *decent* living from their life's work rather than surviving the proverbial "starving artist" lifestyle.

When I founded PPG almost a decade ago, my focus was on "polished publishing." My strategy was to help authors produce professional quality books that could stand proudly beside traditionally-published books, so these books had a better chance of selling. Helping authors with additional book sales and marketing was a secondary service I offered for a sizeable fee.

Now? I still take on publishing business. But my primary focus has shifted to "successful selling." My strategy is to respect every authors' desire for creative freedom by teaching them how to cost-effectively sell their own books, no matter who they've published through—whether that be PPG, another publisher, or independently. I do this through my blog, my books, and online courses which enables me to reach my audience from wherever I am in the world. It allows me to make my *Sales Coaching for Authors* programs affordable for everyone, no matter where you live.

Respecting others' creative freedom, in this way, gives me the creative freedom *I* desire. It allows me to travel and see this beautiful world of ours while I earn a living doing what I love to do most. That's what I've always craved for myself from the start: freedom. Creative, financial, and otherwise. FREEDOM. And I want to help others enjoy the same.

What is *Your* Vision?

If you haven't already done so, send a prayer into the universe and ask for a clear vision of success for your authorship. How will you serve your readers in a way that brings you (and them) a strong sense of fulfillment? What does your perfect writing room look like? Do you see yourself traveling the world or working from home? Can you visualize your books being adapted into film like the Harry Potter or Hunger Games book series were? If yes, who will play the staring role in these movies? Will you attend the premieres? What will you say about your books and your life when you're interviewed? Get specific with your visualizations. Have fun with it. Feel the joy you'll feel when these things happen for real.

> "All you need is your own imagination. So, use it that's what it's for. Go inside for your finest inspiration. Your dreams will open the door."
> ~Madonna, Vogue lyrics

If you still think this isn't possible for you, keep reading. This book is filled with stories of people who started with nothing except a dream and turned it into a reality despite unbelievable odds. Let their life stories act as your proof of what's possible in those moments when you're doubting everything. Keep feeding yourself these positive examples and affirmations while you work toward your goal, and trust that your faith will develop over time. Once it does, you'll be unstoppable.

WHEN YOU COME UP AGAINST RESISTANCE, STAY THE COURSE

When you come up against any resistance along the way—and you *will*—I recommend you read this chapter to remind yourself that you're in good company. You'll find it helps you feel better. Most (if not all) of today's most successful people had to overcome other people's misunderstanding, criticism, or outright opposition to their goals. In fact, even people like Guglielmo Marconi, the Italian inventor of radio communication, came up against some *serious* resistance from those closest to him.

> Marconi dreamed of a system for harnessing the intangible forces of the ether. Evidence that he did not dream in vain may be found in every radio, TV, and cell phone in the world. Moreover, Marconi's dream brought the humblest cabin and the most stately manor house side by side. It made people of every nation on earth next-door neighbors by creating a medium where news, information, and entertainment could instantly be disseminated throughout the world. It may interest you to know that Marconi's "friends" had him taken into custody, and examined in a psychopathic hospital, when he announced he had discovered a principle through which he could send messages through the air, without the aid of wires or other direct physical means of communication. (Hill, 1937)

I think it's safe to say you won't come across quite that extreme of opposition against your own book goals. (At least, I hope not!) My purpose in including Marconi's example—and all the examples listed in this chapter—is simply to show you that you're not alone when you face resistance in the future. Stay the course, as these people did, and you'll eventually fulfill your vision. You may even change the world in the process. Thank God Marconi stayed the course even after those closest to him had him committed for treatment, otherwise we may not be enjoying the benefit of his inventions today. How else would I have the freedom to run a digital publishing company without wireless communication?

Her Lawyer Thought Her Idea Was *So* Bad, He Must Be on Candid Camera

There are several videos posted on YouTube of Sara Blakely giving keynote speeches to either the National Association of Professional Women (NAPW) or The Edge Connection in Atlanta, Georgia, et cetera. I highly recommend watching all of them. She is frank about her total lack of direction in her early career—from two failed attempts at The Law School Admission Test (LSAT), a stint working as a chipmunk at Disney World (after being rejected for the Goofy role), a couple of stand-up comedy gigs, to finally settling on a job selling fax machines for an office supply company called Danka. Sara pokes fun at herself all the way through this story filled with many twists and turns, which puts the rest of us at ease by letting us know it's okay to fail along the way. Everyone does.

In fact, there were many "failures" and rejections along Sara's Spanx journey that would have stopped most people in their tracks. First of all, *nobody* understood her vision of "footless pantyhose" in the beginning; so, even finding a manufacturer who would agree to help her make a prototype was a challenge all on its own. This was because she was dealing mainly with men who couldn't see things through a woman's eyes. And that's when it dawned on her that maybe this was the whole reason why women's shapers and undergarments were so uncomfortable—because they were being created by men who had never worn them before. Luckily, this realization motivated Sara rather than discouraging her. She knew she was going to change the way women wear clothes, and she stayed true to that vision through every trial and tribulation she faced—even despite no formal business education or fashion industry experience.

Sara couldn't even find a female patent attorney in the state of Georgia, so trying to patent her "footless pantyhose" idea proved to be equally trying. Again, she found herself dealing with men who simply couldn't understand her vision. In fact, the attorney who ended up helping her later admitted that he initially thought her idea was so bad it must be a joke. While she was describing it to him in his office that first day, he kept looking around for a hidden camera because he thought he was being pranked for an episode of Candid Camera.

Finally, after several attempts, she found a hosiery mill that would work with her. Why did this one finally come around? Because the man she met with ran her idea by his two daughters; they loved it and begged him to help Sara make it. Finally, some females could see the brilliance of her vision. But that only happened due to Sara's own persistence.

This Young Man Was Thrown in Jail for Pursuing His Goal

The following quote isn't just some formulaic rhetoric that Arnold Schwarzenegger spews to his audience members during keynote speeches. He lives his own life by these words. He walks his talk every day. These five rules are exactly how he has achieved every single one of his goals:

> "Have a vision. Think big. Ignore the naysayers. Work your ass off. And give back and change the world. Because if not us, who? If not now, when?"
> ~Arnold Schwarzenegger

Arnold was faced with many naysayers all through his life, starting with his own friends and family members in Austria. For starters, none of them understood his obsession with bodybuilding because it wasn't a common sport in their part of the world. They teased the 15-year-old relentlessly about his "impossible dreams," and his worried mother even called a doctor to try to make sense of all the pictures of oiled-up muscle men on his bedroom walls. When Arnold turned 18, his abusive alcoholic father gladly sent him off to the military in the hopes it would set his son straight.

Arnold's next big obstacle was trying to figure out how to train every day within the confines of a military base. They didn't have the standard bodybuilding equipment he needed, and they controlled much of his time with military training. He decided not to let anything stop him and challenged himself to work even harder every day. When everyone else around him practically dropped dead from exhaustion in the evenings, Arnold worked out for three more hours. He even woke up earlier than everyone else to get his sit-ups and push-ups done every morning, all the while keeping his vision clear in his mind.

Then one day, he received an invitation to go to the Junior Mr. Europe competition in Stuttgart, Germany. This was his only opportunity to go because, once he turned 19, he would no longer qualify for this competition. Of course, the military would never willingly let Arnold go during basic training. So, after many sleepless nights, he decided he would have to sneak off the base and take a freight train to the event. This turned out to be a good decision in that he made it there in time to compete, and he won first prize! Unfortunately, he was caught a day later trying to sneak back onto the military base; and he was thrown in solitary confinement for several days as punishment.

Imagine the mental games Arnold's mind was playing with him as he sat in jail, pondering his future. But, somehow, he found a way to stay true to his vision even under those extreme conditions. He continued working out on the floor of his cell.

When his superiors finally released him from solitary, they verbally reprimanded him in their office at first. But things turned around when he confirmed for them that he had won the competition he'd gone AWOL to attend. Their anger then turned to pride, and they began using him as an example of strong discipline in front of his peers. They also had body building equipment built for him so he could continue working out every day. Arnold had *finally* won everyone over after three years of going it alone.

From there, he won several more European bodybuilding titles which eventually led to him receiving a literal "ticket to America" from Joe Weider at the age of 21. He trained at Gold's Gym in Los Angeles, California, under Joe's supervision and went on to become the youngest ever Mr. Olympia two years later, at the age of 23.

Next up? Become a Hollywood movie star. This goal proved just as challenging as the first with even more naysayers lined up for him to win over.

When Arnold first began meeting with agents, managers, and studio executives in the movie industry, they literally laughed at him. They all told him it would be impossible for him to become a leading man in Hollywood due to his thick German accent, his over-developed body, and his funny name that was difficult to pronounce. They told him the new "sex symbol" trend of the day was smaller men like Woody Allen, Al Pacino, and Dustin Hoffman. He was told, "Forget about it. You're a nice guy, a fit guy. Why don't you go open up a gym or health food store?" They told him the most he could hope for may be a few bit parts playing a bouncer or maybe a Nazi officer in Hogan's Heroes. That was all he should expect.

But Arnold saw more for himself. He'd already proven to himself, once before, that he could achieve a goal against all odds. He just had to keep his vision clear in his mind while he took daily action toward it. Determined to succeed, he applied the same work ethic and dedication to becoming an actor as he had used to become Mr. Olympia. He started taking acting classes, English classes, speech classes, and even accent removal classes on the side of his full-time work in construction.

Arnold got his first break in 1970 playing Hercules in a movie called Hercules in New York where they recorded another man's voice over his to hide his accent. That was followed by more little television parts and a chance to appear in one of Lucille Ball's specials. Six years later, he appeared in Stay Hungry, then The Streets of San Francisco, then Pumping Iron, et cetera. Finally, he got his big break with Conan the Barbarian—a movie fraught with difficulties and delays that didn't actually premiere in theatres until 1982.

Whenever Arnold speaks about his achievements, he highlights how his personal qualities, that the naysayers had once categorized as liabilities, eventually became his greatest assets. While on a promotional tour, the director of Conan the Barbarian told the press, "If we didn't have Arnold with all his muscles, we would have had to build one." When Arnold later starred in The Terminator, James Cameron expressed gratitude for his accent with this statement: "The 'I'll be back' line became one of the most famous movie lines in history because of Arnold's crazy accent, because he sounded like a machine when he talked."

Arnold faced similar obstacles when he ran for Governor of California years later. Of course, he eventually won that race, too. Didn't he? The rest of his story is history.

This Undiagnosed Dyslexic Started Out Earning Only $25 Per Set

As if living in poverty in a van wasn't a big enough obstacle for the teenage Jim Carrey, there were many more mountains for him to climb on his journey to success. An undiagnosed dyslexic who often struggled in school, he ended up dropping out halfway through grade 10 to help his family make ends meet. But someone without a high school diploma—or even a GED—doesn't have many job options. He could be hired for janitorial or dishwashing jobs, but that was about it.

Imagine how that must have affected his self-esteem and mental health at such a young age.

Jim decided he'd might as well go to the local comedy clubs at night and work on his act for $25 per set. At least it was *some* money, and it allowed him to move toward his vision of freeing other people—perhaps even himself, at that time—from concern. It's hard to believe that his first attempts at doing impressions completely bombed. But Jim stayed the course and honed his talent, spending hours in front of the mirror to perfect his facial expressions.

In his late twenties, he finally landed a recurring role with an American sketch comedy television series called In Living Color. That gave him some national recognition, enabling him to tour and earn more money as a stand-up comedian.

Four years after his In Living Color debut, Jim Carrey completed three movies that made him a multimillionaire: Ace Ventura: Pet Detective (1994), Dumb and Dumber (1994), and The Mask (1994). Now he's a household name. But his journey there was a long one that lasted well over a decade.

Her Teachers Were Mentally Abusive and Her Family Resented Her

If you are ever given the opportunity to listen to Lisa Nichols speak about her past and all the obstacles she had to overcome to get to where she is today, take it. She is living, breathing proof that anything is possible for *anyone* who is willing to work for it. And she is one of the most inspirational authors and sought-after public speakers in the world right now.

But it wasn't always that way for her. Nothing was handed to this self-proclaimed "C Student" in life. Quite the opposite. In school, Lisa's English teacher told her she was the weakest writer she'd ever met in her entire life. That same year, she took a speech class and that teacher recommended she get a desk job and never speak in public. Can you say *cruelty*? These were supposed to be professional *teachers*—people who support and nurture their students.

But the beauty of Lisa Nichols is that she never dwelled on what negative people like that said to her, nor does she hold any grudges toward them to this day. She simply chalks their attitudes up to, "These were demotivated, sad people. Hurt people hurt other people. Sad people make other people sad. Don't take it personal."

Through these teachers and other troubled people in her community, Lisa could see that her only chance at a better life was to leave and find new sources of education and inspiration. During an interview with Tom Bilyeu, she said, "I had to be willing to not only relocate my mind but also relocate my body so I could relocate my finances, relocate my possibilities, and relocate my son's future." And this would be up to her alone since her son's father had landed in prison when their baby was only eight months old.

When Lisa became an avid student of abundance and prosperity, she didn't have a lot of support around her initially. In fact, her new focus caused some resentment and concern among her immediate family members. She told Tom, "I had to go through a window of ten years of judgement: 'You're leaving us, hanging out with white people all the time, going to all these crazy countries...' But I knew I had to be willing to allow my conviction to make me inconvenienced." That's not an easy thing to do, especially when your own family is holding meetings about you—and you're not invited to them!

During that same interview, Lisa said, "Most people want the convenience of transformation without the inconvenience that is required to make that transformation." She was willing to make those inconvenient, radical changes to transform her and her son's life—working harder, sleeping less, leaving her "tribe" to walk on her own path for a while. "The doorway to your new life is for *you* to fit through. You can't carry everybody else through it with you—trying to be their Rescue 911. You have to rescue *you* first." Lisa says she is now much more valuable to her family, and to her community, because she was willing to let them go, walk through that door alone, teach herself, learn a better way of living, and then come back and get them afterward. Her family can now see how much more valuable she is to them, too.

Her College Peers Were Jealous of Her Success and Taunted Her About It

Oprah Winfrey may have gotten some early breaks in her career, but she also had to suffer through similar resentment and criticism as Lisa Nichols did. The most hurtful taunting came from her college peers when she was a young and insecure nineteen-year-old.

> **32.35 location on video:** And I started to read. Now, I've been reading since I was three. They couldn't believe how well I read, and I was hired. There. So, when somebody said, 'Sit down and read' and they said 'Come hear this girl read!' And someone else came, and before I knew it, there

were four guys standing in the room listening to me read. And I was hired, 17 years old, in radio. At the time, I was still a senior [in high school], so I had to only work after school. So, I'd finish, get there by 3:30, and I'd do on-the-air newscasts. Well, all my friends just hated me because they're cutting grass. And, um, my sophomore year in college, someone heard me on the radio and said, 'We heard you on the radio, would you be interested in working in television.' And I turned them down three times. And the third time, I had a college professor, I said, 'They keep calling me to be on television. And I know if I do television, I'll never finish school.' So, he said, 'Don't you know that's why people *go* to school? So that somebody can keep calling them, you nitwit!' So, I went, and I interviewed for the job [in television] … I was 19 at the time, so I decided to pretend to be Barbara Walters because that's how I'd gotten into this in the first place. So, I sat there, pretending with Barbara in my head, did everything I thought she would do, and I was hired. It was amazing. As a matter of fact, it was because of the riots of the 70s that I think they were looking for minorities. They were trying to fulfill all of their quotas and programs, and so I was hired as a token and had to take the heat from my college classmates. I went to an all-black college with them calling me a token. … And I was very defensive about it because I've always had to live with the notion of other black people saying, for any amount of success that you achieve, they say, 'Oh, you're trying to be white. You're trying to talk white. You're trying to be white.' And so forth. Which is such a ridiculous notion to me since you look in the mirror every morning and you're black. There's a black face in your reflection. So, I had to live with that whole thing. ... And it was very uncomfortable for me at first because when I first started as a broadcaster, I was 19. Very insecure, thrown into television, pretending to be Barbara Walters, looking nothing like her, and still going to college. So, I would do all my classes in the morning from eight to one. And in the afternoon, I'd work from two to 10 and do the six o'clock news. And would stay up and study and all that stuff, you know, until one, two, or three o'clock in the morning. Then just start the routine all over again. (Winfrey)

She obviously had an amazing work ethic from a very young age, and that has continued throughout her life. But she also had her obstacles to overcome, just like the rest of us.

This Italian Actor Couldn't Even Get Cast for a Bit Part ... as an *Italian*

Sylvester Stallone was so driven by his desire to help other people escape, and to inspire them to achieve what they're capable of in life, that he was unwilling to settle for anything else. For a long time, he was the epitome of the "starving artist." He didn't want to get a "real job" because he knew if he *did*, he'd get seduced back into "the real world" and lose the hunger he had for his dream. He felt his hunger was his greatest advantage, and he turned out to be right about that.

Audition after audition, Sylvester was turned down for acting parts. He once told Tony Robbins that he was thrown out more than 1,500 times from various agents' offices in New York. In fact, he was once even turned down for a bit part as an Italian in The Godfather. He asked, "What part of me didn't pass the Italian identification aspect?" They never gave him a straight answer why. Just imagine what *that* did to his psyche!

Sylvester persisted despite all this rejection and got a few parts here and there. He also sold a script he'd written, titled Paradise Alley, for $100. That gave him some hope. But none of it ever led to solid work and his financial struggles continued. Eventually, he was *so* broke that he had to sell his beloved dog, Butkus, because he couldn't afford to feed him. In several interviews, he has said that was one of the lowest moments of his life.

One night, not long after he sold his dog (for only $25 … *ouch!*), Sylvester watched a match between boxing legend Muhammad Ali and Chuck Wepner that inspired him to write the first draft of his future-Oscar-winning Rocky script. For him, that fight was a metaphor—not only for a man who takes his shot and goes the distance with a true champion, but who also stands up to life. That was who the character in his new script, Rocky Balboa, was to him. It is also the essence of Sylvester Stallone himself. Unfortunately, he would have to fight many more rounds to sell that script and get the movie made on his terms.

It wasn't enough for him to sell this script to a producer as he'd done with Paradise Alley; Sylvester also wanted to be cast in the leading role. Although he was able to find some producers who loved the script, nobody wanted to hire *him* as Rocky Balboa at first. They wanted to put an established star in that role, instead—someone like Ryan O'Neal.

Back and forth, the negotiations continued. These producers went from offering him $25,000 to $100,000 to

$150,000 to $175,000 to $250,000 to $330,000 for the rights to produce Rocky with a different actor in the starring role. Despite how broke he was, Sylvester kept turning them down. He knew what he *truly* wanted—which was to star in this movie—and he refused to compromise. Luckily, these producers eventually gave in. They brought their offer back down to $35,000, along with points in the movie, in exchange for casting Sylvester as the leading man. He agreed to the reduced rate and willingly assumed all risk along with them. This turned out to be a very profitable gamble because Rocky grossed $200,000,000 at the box office although it only cost them $1,000,000 to produce.

You may find it pleasing to learn that, as soon as Sylvester was paid the $35,000, he went in search of the man he'd sold his dog to. He found him and bought Butkus back from him. He even gave that man and his dog bit parts in the first Rocky movie. Doesn't that make you smile?

I Went to the Edge of the Cliff … and It Crumbled Out from Under Me

Will Smith and Lisa Nichols often encourage others to face their fears of the unknown head on—to go to the proverbial edge of the cliff and jump. Just jump! Because on the other side of your fear of falling is where you'll find all your dreams and your bliss.

"God placed the best things in life on the other side of terror," Will assures you. "On the other side of your maximum fears are all of the best things in life."

"Your brain is designed to keep you safe. Your soul, your intuition, your human spirit is designed to make you soar," Lisa will tell you. "When you get to the edge, your brain will always tell you to step back. It's always going to tell you to step back because you could fall. It's designed to keep you safe. So, you have to be willing to play between your brain and your soul. And, on some days, you've got to just listen to your soul. You've got to leap."

When I came home from my Asian adventure in 2016, I decided to take Will's and Lisa's advice. As I mentioned in *The Author's Money Tree*, I didn't go back to a "real job" straightaway because I wanted to turn off the corporate noise and *really* focus on my craft. I found four personal investors to help me cover my expenses while I focused. In other words, I went to the edge of that cliff in the form of taking on significant debt without any guaranteed income coming into my household to offset it. I had faith the money would come to me in droves if I gave 100% effort to my vision and worked toward it daily.

What was the result of my little experiment? Two things happened: one, I achieved my first goal of *finally* figuring out how authors can earn a decent living from their books; but, two, before I could reach my second goal of earning a decent living from my own books, the edge of that cliff crumbled out from under me. In short, I stayed there too long, the money ran out, and then it took me another three and a half months to find employment. So, I didn't get a chance to jump *or* soar. Instead, I took a serious tumble that sent me on a financial rollercoaster ride for about two years. I was forced to find *two* new jobs, and work *seven* days per week, to recover from that fall and re-stabilize my finances.

It was humiliating; I'm not going to lie to you. It was so discouraging to reach such heights in my life only to fall back down so hard. You see, things had been on a financial upswing for me just before this happened. Not only had I enjoyed several trips during the previous three years; but, just before I got home from Asia, I'd also received an email from the team at TheSecret.tv informing me that my personal "Story of the Week" was going to be featured in Rhonda Byrne's upcoming book titled *How The Secret Changed My Life: Real People. Real Stories.* This was an absolute dream come true for me—yet another affirmation that all my actions and visualizations were paying off. It strengthened my faith that I *could* safely stand on the edge of that cliff. I *could* jump. And I *would* soar. It was the whole reason I decided to do it.

But then it all came crumbling down. During these past two years, I haven't had much of a social life—never mind any opportunities to travel. I haven't had much sleep, either; I've been too busy rebuilding. After much contemplation, I can now see the blessing in disguise. Being grounded in this way, after learning the key to success for authors, has strengthened my focus and improved my work ethic. Along with holding two jobs, I've also written and published 35 new books over the past two years—all without burning out or losing interest in the task at hand.

I have an energy that I didn't have before because I know how to do this now. I know it's possible, so I'm perfectly okay with doing the necessary work. By taking that time to focus solely on my vision, I gained something far greater than an immediate increase in my personal book sales. I came away with more stamina—an even *stronger* faith— than I had before. And that's what this whole book is about: developing one's faith to a point where you'll be able to overcome any obstacle you face. Because there will always be obstacles and difficulties to contend with.

You're going to make mistakes along the way. If you want to succeed in life, you have to be *willing* to fail. Will Smith put it perfectly when he said this:

> **0:01 location on video:** Fail early. Fail often. Fail forward. It's always a little bit frustrating to me when people have a negative relationship with failure. Failure is a massive part of being able to be successful. You have to get comfortable with failure. You have to actually seek failure. Because failure is where all of the lessons are.
>
> When you go to the gym and you work out, you're actually seeking failure. You want to take your muscles to the point where you get to failure because that's where the adaptation is. That's where the growth is.
>
> Successful people fail a lot. They fail a whole lot more than they succeed, but they extract the lessons from the failure, and they use that—they use the energy, and they use the wisdom—to come around to the next phase of success.
>
> You've got to take a shot. You have to live at the edge of your capabilities. You've got to live where you're almost certain that you're going to fail. (Smith)

That's how you succeed. You already know this instinctively because that's how we all learned to walk when we were babies—by *failing* and falling, over and over again, until the day finally came when we could stand on our own two feet.

So, go to the edge of that cliff. Jump. Soar. Or, fall flat on your face as I did. Own it. Learn from it. Apologize and fix it, if the situation calls for it. Then move forward with increased faith.

No matter what, you'll be fine so long as you get back up again and keep moving forward. I can assure you that I'm fine. I'm still here. And I'm still willing and able to fail forward toward my version of success.

What Are You Telling Yourself About *Your* Obstacles?

You might be telling yourself, "Well, *they* can all do it, but I can't because…." And your mind may be feeding you all kinds of excuses and seemingly legitimate reasons why. If that's the case, I invite you to delve further into the study of faith. Read the books and watch the videos of the people I've introduced you to here. You'll begin to see that they're just like you; you're just like them.

> "Nothing was ever in any man that is not in you; no man ever had more spiritual or mental power than you can attain, or did greater things than you can accomplish. You can become what you want to be."
> ~Wallace D. Wattles

It will not happen overnight. In fact, it may take months or even years to accomplish your goals. But time doesn't really matter when you're doing what you love, does it? Because when you're doing what you love, it doesn't feel like work at all.

HOW MUCH TIME WILL IT TAKE?

How much time it takes to reach your dream is dependent on how much deliberate action, focused thought, and dedicated faith you feed it on a consistent basis. As I mentioned in book one of this series, it took Joanna Penn five years to transition into being a full-time writer and another four to earn a six-figure income from it. By contrast, it took Amanda Hocking about two years to transition from an $18,000 annual income, earned from taking care of severely disabled people, to becoming a millionaire from self-publishing her paranormal fiction series.

Everyone's journey to success is a little different, so I can't give you a definitive answer on how long it will take you. I can only show you case studies and share other people's strategies with you. They all seem to follow a similar formula as you can see by reading their stories.

It Took a Little Over Two Years for Her Invention to be Recognized Nationally

From the time Sara Blakely first cut the feet out of her control-top pantyhose, through the process of getting the prototype made, coming up with the perfect name of Spanx, designing her logo and packaging, to finally launching her product in Neiman Marcus stores was a two-year period. This was all done in her spare time, on weekends and weekday evenings, while she continued working full-time for Danka.

Some people may think that, once her product was in Neiman Marcus, it must have been smooth sailing from there. Nothing could be further from the truth. According to Sara, that's when the *real* work began, and she had to ensure the product was moving so the retailers would keep it in-store. She didn't have any money for advertising, so she had to rely on her own work ethic and sales abilities to ensure people kept buying Spanx.

Sara continued visualizing her goals while working toward them, and one of her top visualizations was being interviewed by Oprah about her invention. She sent a basketful of her products to The Oprah Winfrey Show and kept the faith that this would provide her with the big break she needed. It certainly did. Oprah named Spanx as one of her "favourite things" in November of 2000—a little more than two years after Sara first invented it. Then, and only then, did she quit her full-time job at Danka. It took another decade of hard work for Sara Blakely to be recognized as a self-made billionaire in *Forbes* magazine.

His First Goal Took Six Years to Achieve and His Second Took Twice as Long

Arnold Schwarzenegger's vision began to develop very early in his life, when he first saw that video of America in school at around the age of 10. But he didn't set a concrete plan as to how he would get to America until he was 15 years old and read that article about Reg Park; so, I'll start his official count-down from age 15.

It took Arnold until he was 21 years old to achieve his first goal of moving to America. That's six solid years. And it took 12 years, from his first role in Hercules in New York in 1970, to when he got his big break in the movie business with Conan the Barbarian in 1982.

Arnold is a role model for so many things—two of them being patience and tenacity. He *never* gave up, no matter how long it took him to reach his goals. That's why he eventually succeeded at all of them. So, if you ever come across someone who is criticizing *your* goals with, "It's taking too long. That must be a sign it won't happen for you," just remember Arnold's example. Ignore the naysayers who think you should give up. Adjust your course a bit whenever you have to. But never quit.

He Attracted $10,000,000 to Himself Within Three Years

When Jim Carrey finally landed his recurring role on the television show In Living Color, that may have been the first time he was able to see past his lifetime of financial struggles. Because, as he told Oprah Winfrey during an interview in February of 1997, that was around the time he made his first big financial wish. He told her that he used to spend evenings at the scenic overlook up on Mulholland Drive in Los Angeles. While there, he would visualize having movie directors interested in him and people that he respected telling him that they liked his work.

At this time, he also wrote himself a cheque for $10,000,000 "for acting services rendered" and gave himself three years, until Thanksgiving 1995, to make this financial wish come true. He kept that cheque in his wallet as he continued to visualize his dreams every night. Jim told Oprah, "Just before Thanksgiving 1995, I found out that I was going to make $10,000,000 on the movie Dumb and Dumber."

To which Oprah replied, "Visualization works if you work hard."

And Jim agreed, "You can't just visualize and then go eat a sandwich."

The most beautiful part of Jim Carrey's story is that, when his father passed away, he put that cheque into his casket with him. It had been his father's greatest wish for Jim to realize their shared dream of becoming a great comedian; that man had been one of his son's biggest cheerleaders through it all.

She Grew Her Bank Account from $11.42 to $62,500 in Three and a Half Years

In 1996, Lisa Nichols was a struggling single mom on government assistance, with only $11.42 in her bank account. By 2016, twenty years later, she was a multimillionaire entrepreneur. Along that winding road to long-term success, she accomplished many other short-term goals.

One of Lisa's short-term goals had to do with reframing her relationship with money—how to earn it, how to keep it, how to grow it—so she would never be that broke or broken again. She did this by scaling back the unnecessary expenses in her life (e.g., going out for dinner, getting her nails done) and putting that money into a savings account each pay day, instead. For three and a half years, Lisa invested in herself in this way, increasing the percentage she saved by 5% each month. This was how she increased her bank account balance from $11.42 to $62,500 and was able to fund her dream of motivating others to improve their lives as she had improved her own. Back then, she started by motivating teenagers. Now, she motivates the masses!

It Took Her One Decade to Turn Her Dream into Reality

Oprah may have started her television career at the young age of nineteen, but it took another thirteen years before The Oprah Winfrey Show was nationally syndicated in 1986—shortly after she was cast as Sofia in the movie The Color Purple. Considering she had wanted to be an actress since at least her early twenties, it took her around one decade of work and visualizing to make that dream come true for herself.

He Lived in Poverty for Eight Years Until His Big Break Came

Sylvester Stallone was 30 years old when the first Rocky movie was launched in theatres. But he'd already been trying to break into movies for several years at that point. Based on his IMDb webpage, his first role was in "a picture story at an LSD party on the beach" (whatever *that* is) in 1969 called The Square Foot. After that, he was hired for a few minor roles as either a "stud" or a "thug" in various other films until, at long last, his Rocky dream came true in 1976. But it was a long haul for Sylvester, and he lived in poverty through all of it.

It Has Taken Me 25 Years of Trial and Error to Write This Book

Since as far back as I can remember, I've wanted to be an author, but not just any old author. I've wanted to be a *bestselling* author. It was a long and educational journey to the achievement of this goal that, once realized, still didn't allow me to earn a living from my writing. That was rather anticlimactic after putting in so much time and effort.

In 2013, I wrote and published my first official bestseller, titled *How to Publish a Book in Canada ... and Sell Enough Copies to Make a Profit!*, that discussed the merits of professional book publishing. With close to 20 years' experience in the industry, I had a strong understanding of the pros and cons of each book publishing business model (e.g., traditional trade publishing, "hybrid" supported self-publishing, and "vanity" self-publishing), and I knew what it took to create a bestseller. Still, my faith in the average author's ability—including my own—to earning a decent *living* from writing was still weak. My results reflected that frail confidence in all areas.

Three years ago, I took a hiatus from my disillusioned dream to clear my head. When I returned home from my Asian "eat pray love" working holiday six months later, I felt refreshed and ready to try again. That's when I changed my focus from earning some fruitless title to earning a decent living from my craft. I realized that my goal—my true passion—had always been about *freedom* and *travel*. And as long as I had to work full-time elsewhere to earn a living, then my freedom to travel would remain limited by someone else's rules and expectations.

Once I homed in on the *true* essence of my dream, I was able to focus and find the solutions that had long eluded me. It has taken me 25 years of trial and error to write this book. But that's okay. I've never felt more exhilarated than I do today!

How Long Will It Take You?

As you can see, from reading all the examples in this chapter, everyone's road to success is a little different. The time it takes to achieve a goal can vary. How long will it take you? I don't have an answer for you. My only advice is to never give up. Find your own passion as an author, and then work toward it each and every day. Your sense of purpose will keep you energized and feeling enthusiastic about your dream.

SUCCESS LEAVES CLUES (WORK ETHIC AND SLEEP HABITS)

I am sharing with you the final summary of a book published in 1910 by Wallace D. Wattles before I return to our case studies to share their respective work ethics and sleep habits with you. I think you'll agree, once you read this, they are all indeed following this formula. If it can work for them, it can work for you.

> There is a thinking stuff from which all things are made, and which, in its original state, permeates, penetrates, and fills the interspaces of the universe.
>
> A thought in this substance produces the thing that is imaged by the thought.
>
> Man can form things in his thought, and by impressing his thought upon formless substance can cause the thing he thinks about to be created.
>
> In order to do this, man must pass from the competitive to the creative mind; otherwise he cannot be in harmony with the Formless Intelligence, which is always creative and never competitive in spirit.
>
> Man may come into full harmony with the Formless Substance by entertaining a lively and sincere gratitude for the blessings it bestows upon him. Gratitude unifies the mind of man with the intelligence of Substance, so that man's thoughts are received by the Formless. Man can remain upon the creative plane only by uniting himself

with the Formless Intelligence through a deep and continuous feeling of gratitude.

Man must form a clear and definite mental image of the things he wishes to have, to do, or to become; and he must hold this mental image in his thoughts, while being deeply grateful to the Supreme that all his desires are granted to him. … Too much stress cannot be laid on the importance of frequent contemplation of the mental image, coupled with unwavering faith and devout gratitude. This is the process by which the impression is given to the Formless, and the creative forces set in motion.

The creative energy works through the established channels of natural growth, and of the industrial and social order. All that is included in his mental image will surely be brought to the man who follows the instructions given above, and whose faith does not waver. What he wants will come to him through the ways of established trade and commerce.

In order to receive his own when it shall come to him, man must be active; and this activity can only consist in more than filling his present place. … And he must do, every day, all that can be done that day, taking care to do each act in a successful manner. He must give to every man a use value in excess of the cash value he receives, so that each transaction makes for more life; and he must so hold the Advancing Thought that the impression of increase will be communicated to all with whom he comes into contact. (Wattles, 1910)

Let's use sunlight as an analogy for a moment. If it is spread thin, it can brighten up a room and warm the air. But if you focus it onto one spot with a magnifying glass, it can cause an intense enough heat to start a fire. Its power becomes much stronger with more focus. The same can be said for the level of focus these individuals each gave to their own dreams—and to the level of success they were each able to achieve as a result of that intense focus.

> **2:48 location on video:** I realize that to have the level of success that I want to have is difficult to spread it out and do multiple things. It takes such a desperate, obsessive focus. You've really got to focus with all of your fibre, and all of your heart, and all of your creativity. (Smith2)

Will Smith isn't the only one who advocates intense focus. Here's what Napoleon Hill has to say about it.

> "Your ability to use the principal of autosuggestion will depend, very largely, upon your capacity to *concentrate* upon a given *desire* until that desire becomes a *burning obsession*."
> ~Napoleon Hill

In other words, if your family members start telling you, "I'm worried about you. You seem a little obsessed," then smile to yourself. Because you're probably on track to achieving great things.

She Spent *Countless* Hours on the Road Promoting Her Brand

Sara Blakely is a workhorse. I'm unable to find specific information regarding her sleep habits, but everything I *can* find on her tells me she worked her butt off daily—and still does—to ensure her company's success. As it is with most start-ups, she had to be and do everything in the beginning. She was the inventor, manufacturer, sales person, fulfillment and shipping clerk, travel coordinator, marketer, et cetera, while she ran her company out of her apartment for the first couple of years.

Once Sara was able to hire a bit of staff to manage the administrative office work for her, she spent the next couple of years on the road. Seven days per week, she visited the Neiman Marcus stores that carried her products and promoted her Spanx brand to their customers in person. She also continued to cold call other retailers and media outlets at this time. Sara was absolutely determined to ensure her own success, so she left nothing to chance. She held morning rallies with the staff at all these stores to get them pumped up about her product—which was the equivalent of building a sales force that wasn't on her payroll. All across the country, these retail employees eventually became her biggest Spanx advocates along with her own paid staff.

To give you an idea of how much work Sara had to do, each and every day, as she drove around the country selling her products in-store, this was back in the time when nobody had iPhones, iPads, or Blackberries. It was also at a time when the MapQuest website was just becoming popular; so, that was the tool she had to use on each hotel's computer to try to find all the locations she would be driving to each day. She spent a lot of time alone on the road. It was no easy task to build her company, but the passion she felt for her dream carried her through.

This Man Says "Sleep Faster" to Those Who Think They Need Eight Hours

In response to people who try to tell him they don't have the time to do everything they want to do in a day, Arnold Schwarzenegger always replies, "There are 24 hours in a day. You sleep for six of those. That gives you 18 hours to fit everything in." And to the people who try to correct him by saying they need eight hours of sleep every night, he always says, "Sleep faster." I love that line. It makes me smile every time I hear him say it.

Arnold used every last minute of the 18 hours he had available to him every day. *Every* day. When he came to the USA, he continued training five hours a day. To earn his living, he worked as a brick-layer on the side. He went to college and worked to improve his English skills. Plus, he took acting classes every night from 8 PM to midnight. He did that every day to show the Universe how serious he was about achieving his dreams. Look where that got him.

He Worked All Day and Well into the Night for Weeks on End

Jim Carrey's dad first took him to a Yuk Yuk's comedy club in Toronto when he was 15 years old, encouraging him to participate in open mic night. The two of them had written his first comedy act together. That evening, the owner of the club heckled him to the point where Jim almost gave up on stand-up comedy altogether; he didn't return there for two full years. During this hiatus, his patient father kept encouraging him to go back, and they worked together to hone his act.

At age 17, Jim gave stand-up another *serious* try at Yuk Yuk's. This time, he did quite well with his impressions in particular—which makes sense considering he had spent untold hours perfecting them in front of his mirror at home. How many hours did he work on his craft? I found the answer I was searching for in a Rolling Stone article titled "Jim Carrey: Bare Facts and Shocking Revelations" via this one, concise sentence:

> The Carrey who would spend eight hours before a set of mirrors perfecting faces, the Carrey who can't stop himself from working all day and well into the night for weeks on end, is no stranger to darkness and compulsion. (Schruers, 1995)

This level of passion and work ethic is what catapulted Jim Carrey to levels of success he could only have imagined at age 15. Maybe, in some twisted way, that Yuk Yuk's club owner did the teenage a favour but heckling him in such a harsh manner that evening. Perhaps, that made Jim work even harder than he otherwise would have. The rewards for doing so were great.

This Single Parent Found a Way to Ensure Her Son's Bright Future

As a single parent, Lisa Nichols had less time on her hands than child-free individuals do. But she *still* found a way to do the work that was necessary to relocate her and her son's future.

> "*I* am my rescue. Nobody else."
> ~Lisa Nichols

I wish I'd read Lisa's story back when I was a single parent. My son and I may have had more opportunities/luxuries in our lives had I thought, for even a minute, that was possible for us. I now know it *is* possible no matter who you are, no matter what your circumstance is. Lisa is living, breathing proof of it. And she totally hits the mark when she talks about why her example is so powerful for others who are clinging to any shame or regret they may feel about things from the past: "Your story is not meant to be your fortress; your story is meant to be your fuel. The beauty of me being one of the top one percent earners in America is that I was once on government assistance. It wouldn't be a big deal if my family was rich."

Getting to where she is today took *years* of dedication, work, and sacrifice. She started out by using her bedroom closet as her office for the first four years. She used the clip hangers normally used for dress pants to hang all her client files in this little closet office. Back then, she worked full-time at Los Angeles Unified School District while her son was at daycare during the day. Her work day started at 8 AM. After a nine-hour day, she'd pick Jelani up and take him home where she'd enjoy a 30-minute dinner break with him at six o'clock. Then Lisa would work on her own business from six-thirty to midnight every evening. Her son would play beside her while she worked until it was his bedtime.

If Lisa's work day started at 8 AM, that means she was getting up at around 6:30 or 7 AM to get ready each day. She was living off around six and a half to seven hours of sleep every night.

When Jelani was school age, Lisa put him into a private school that allowed her to take him with her whenever she travelled for work. The school would send homework with him on the road; Lisa would help him with that homework in the evenings and then send it back to the school by FedEx®. This woman worked her ass off to fund her own dream and ensure her son's bright future. Ask

Jelani if he feels he missed out on anything due to her work ethic, and I'm sure he'll tell you no. He knows just how much he has gained from it.

This Woman Feels Most Comfortable Working 14 to 16 Hours Per Day

Two chapters ago, you read Oprah Winfrey's own words about the hours she put into school, homework, and work during her senior high school and college years. She has continued that work ethic to this day.

> **1:02:20 location on video:** "14-hour days. 15. A 12-hour day is a short day for me. I feel like, after a 12-hour day, what am I going to do with the rest of my day? I get home, I don't know what to do with myself because I have all of this time left over. I don't know what to do. So, really, I feel most comfortable working 14 to 16 hours. Because then at least I can go home, usually I take a bubble bath. I love bubbles. That's the one big luxury I've given myself, is that now that I have attained some material success, I will use an entire half a bottle of bubble bath at one time. Really extravagant." (Winfrey)

This woman's work ethic is much like Arnold Schwarzenegger's in that she seems to average only six hours of sleep each night. Do the math. If she's working 16 hours per day, and she's spending another two hours on things like dinner and commuting to/from work, that leaves six hours for sleep. She obviously loves what she does to be able to maintain this schedule.

His Three-Day Writing Frenzy Earned $200,000,000

I haven't been able to find any articles or videos specific to his sleep habits. But, whenever Sylvester Stallone talks about watching that match between boxing legend Muhammad Ali and Chuck Wepner, and then feeling inspired to write that first draft of Rocky, he speaks of it being a passionate "writing frenzy" over a period of three days. That three-day writing frenzy, combined with several more months of passionate activity, ultimately earned $200,000,000 at the box office. Three inspired writing days. Barely any sleep. $200,000,000.

She Danced Her Way to Becoming the Most Watched Woman in the World

As a teenager in the 1980s, I was obsessed with everything about Madonna from her fashion to her music videos. I was especially mesmerized whenever I watched her dance. Years later, when I saw a documentary about her titled Driven: Madonna, I learned I wasn't the only one who felt this way about her. So many others were equally hypnotized by her energy on the dance floor—even her high school teachers. When she took to the floor at high school dances, people would clear a space so they could all stand around and watch her. And Madonna loved putting on a show for them.

In this documentary, a guidance counsellor from Madonna's high school, named Nancy Mitchell, talks about how she worked harder than any of the other students did: "The thing I believe that set Madonna apart from many of the other talented kids in school was that she worked longer and harder at her dance. She was the student who got in the car, drove 25 miles to Detroit while all of the other kids were maybe out goofing around, and she was doing dance and practicing for endless hours." Other teachers were convinced Madonna would one day become a professional dancer on Broadway. They all knew she was going *somewhere* great, wherever that may be.

Madonna would go to clubs in Detroit with some of her dance teachers in the evenings. There, she got exposed to new dance moves, people, and lifestyles. After high school, she followed her favourite ballet instructor and mentor, Christopher Flynn, to the University of Michigan on a dance scholarship. This is where she met Whitley Setrakian who became her college roommate. Even Whitley describes the same drive and work ethic that Nancy Mitchell mentioned earlier: "A night after we'd been out dancing and got home at two or three in the morning, she'd be up at eight o'clock in the morning, back out the door, and in the dance department." Madonna was truly disciplined and focused on becoming a professional dancer.

That was, at least, until she became bored with it. Madonna didn't like wasting time, so the idea of spending four years to get a degree was becoming less and less attractive to her. She loved *attention* more than dance itself. She loved being watched and performing for others. So, she decided to move to New York City where she could make a much bigger mark on the world than she ever could in Detroit, Michigan. It was there that Madonna developed her vision to become a world renown entertainer—to become the most famous (most "watched") woman in the world. She put the same level of energy and focus into her new passion as she'd always put into dance, and it obviously paid off.

With Madonna, it was never "I'm going to do this" or "I'm going to be this." Right from the start, it was "I *am* this already." Ask people who knew her back then, and they'll say she lived her vision into existence very quickly by acting as though it was already reality.

As a teenager in the 1980s, I was (and still am) so grateful to Madonna for pursing her dream of being watched. I love the beautiful alchemy of her dream—that someone who others love watching also loves being watched by them. That's the power of love, right there. In my opinion, Madonna's success epitomizes the power of *love*.

His Legacy Is the Epitome of Greatness

If you love reading and watching biographies as much as I do, then you'll love JFK: Like No Other. Despite the fact that John Fitzgerald "Jack" Kennedy came from one of America's wealthiest families, all early indicators showed there was *no* reason why this man should have become the 35th President of the United States. And, despite the financial help he got from his father, plus the campaign help he got from all his family members, it still would never have happened without his own focused work ethic and love of politics.

This person suffered from *serious* health problems that would have stopped most people in their tracks, giving them legitimate excuses to rest rather than push forward: scarlet fever, whooping cough, ongoing digestive ailments caused by colitis, Addison's disease, and chronic back pain. In fact, over his lifetime, JFK received the Catholic sacrament of last rites on four different occasions. That's how sick he was. Add to that the fact that he was filthy stinking rich by inheritance; he never *had* to work a day in his life if he didn't want to.

But JFK was driven and focused on success. Some say he lived his life as though he knew his time was limited, making the most out of each and every day. I believe that's the number one reason he reached the heights he reached during his short life.

In between his bedridden hospital stays, Jack travelled the world, attended Harvard University, and wrote a thesis titled *Appeasement at Munch* that was later published as *Why England Slept*. The book went on to become a bestseller and showed his early interest and understanding of the global political arena. JFK's poor health made it near impossible for him to get past military doctors, so his father had to pull some strings for him to be able to join the navy. This enabled him to take command of a PT boat which led to him becoming a war hero—another impressive credential toward his future political career, but an experience that exacerbated his back problems. From that time forward, JFK needed a back brace and strong medications to manage his pain for the rest of his life.

It's hard to believe now but, when John Kennedy first entered politics, he resembled a scrawny teenager and was a shy, unpolished public speaker. He had to work at improving his public image daily, all while privately managing his health issues. To accomplish this feat, he campaigned from sunrise to midnight each day, climbing the stairs of three-decker buildings to knock on doors and talk to people, all while wearing his canvas-covered steel back brace. Most people would struggle to manage that pace with perfect health. That's what makes JFK's story so inspirational to me, despite all his reported sexual transgressions. His legacy—his image—is the epitome of what it takes to achieve greatness. Jack apparently kept up this pace to the very end of his life.

Writing During His Commute Earned This Author $450,000 in One Year

I can't find any articles specific to Mark Dawson's sleep habits. But I did come across one of his podcasts (SPF-076: The Science of Sleep and How It Can Help Your Writing Career – with Dr. Anne Bartolucci) that discusses the importance of sleep for creative minds, and how a brain needs adequate sleep to function well enough to be able to create anything. That said, what exactly constitutes "an adequate-enough sleep" that will allow you to be as productive and creative as someone like Mark?

> How does he maintain such a high release-rate? By using his four-hour daily commute to London to write thousands of words a day. As soon as he sits down on the train and opens up his laptop, he's writing solidly until it's time to get off. (McGregor, 2017)

For whatever reason, so many of us have this misguided notion that *everyone* needs eight hours of sleep per night in order to function properly during the day. But, according to Dr. Anne Bartolucci, sleep needs actually vary between individuals. While she says she needs around eight hours of sleep each night, she acknowledges that her husband only needs around six. In fact, if he gets too much sleep for him (e.g., eight hours per night) for too many days in a row, it turns into insomnia.

Obviously, if Mark Dawson was having to commute four hours each day for work, plus working an eight-hour day, he was living off—and being highly productive on—only around six hours of sleep per night. I say that because you have to give him at least another six waking hours per day for meals, family time, and all the additional activities involved in successful book publishing.

Her Frenzy of Focused Activity Precipitated Million-dollar Book Sales

I've often wondered why Amanda Hocking was able to become a multimillionaire so quickly compared to most other independent authors. Then, one day, it hit me as I was researching the work ethic and sleep habits of my most cherished mentors-from-afar. I noticed something I hadn't noticed before, and I would like to share it with you here. It is a portion of the Ed Pilkington article in The Guardian, titled "Amanda Hocking, the writer who made millions by self-publishing online," that I've mentioned beforehand.

> In 2009 she went into overdrive. She was frantic to get her first book published by the time she was 26, the age Stephen King was first in print, and time was running out (she's now 27). So while holding down a day job caring for severely disabled people, for which she earned $18,000 a year, she went into a Red Bull-fuelled frenzy of writing at night, starting at 8pm and continuing until dawn. Once she got going, she could write a complete novel in just two or three weeks. By the start of 2010, she had amassed a total of 17 unpublished novels, all gathering digital dust on the desktop of her laptop. (Pilkington, 2012)

This frenzy of focused activity—working all day at her full-time job followed by writing all evening and late into the night—seems to be what precipitated the mass sales of her books once she published them a year later. Coincidence? Maybe. Maybe not.

Sleep Doesn't Create Energy. *Faith* Does.

My conclusion, from all my research, is that there is something ethereal to this sleep thing—or, specifically, this *obsessed* level of focused productivity during one's waking hours. The more I study other successful people, the more I realize prayer is received by God (or the Universe, or whatever you call it) through your *actions* more so than your thoughts. It is only when you combine massive action, grateful thoughts, and a strong feeling of faith together that your prayers are fully heard and finally answered.

> "The answer to prayer is not according to your faith while you are talking, but according to your faith while you are working."
> ~Wallace D. Wattles

We all need enough sleep. But energy doesn't come from enough sleep; it comes from feeling a strong desire for something and a faith that you can achieve it. I learned that firsthand, over these past two years, when I published 35 books while working two jobs simultaneously. Where that pace would have burned me out in the past, I can easily maintain it now—because I know how to do this now. I know it's possible. I have faith.

> **15:20 location on video:** We're not made for work. Work's made for us. What we've got to do is find out what we *love*, and then you have to do it because you *love* it. … See, when people quit—like Three Feet from Gold—they weren't in love with that idea. They were going after the money. It

wasn't the idea that motivated them; it was the money that motivated them, and that's why they quit. ... That's one of the big problems with people when they set goals. They set a goal to do what they think they can do. Well, there's no inspiration in that. It's got to be what you *want* to do. ... When you're going after your heart's desire, you don't quit. ... You see, you don't *get* energy. All the energy there ever was or ever will be is omnipresent. It's evenly present in all places at the same time. You don't *get* energy; you *release* energy. You're just an instrument that energy flows through. Desire is the triggering mechanism that releases the energy. When you've got the desire, you've got the energy. When you haven't got any desire, you haven't got any energy. (Proctor, 2017)

This is what Wallace D. Wattles is referring to when he says you must "do each act in a *successful* manner." Your dream needs to inspire you. The actions you take need to energize you—and they *will* when they are infused with grateful thoughts and a strong feeling of faith. When you combine these three things—action, thought, and faith—in most every act you take toward your dream, then most every act you take will be successful. Your dream as a whole will be successful.

I Have Far More Energy Due to This Change in my Sleeping Habits

My mother is a wonderful, caring person. She's also a nurse whose health advice I've heeded all my life. My mother was (and still is) a strong advocate of a "good night's sleep." But, looking back, that was taken to extremes when I was a child. I was in bed at 8 PM and slept for 12 hours until 8 AM seven days per week. She also made sure I had a two-hour nap every afternoon. That means I was asleep for 14 hours per day, every day, for the first five years of my life. I slept more than half my life away at that time.

Long sleep hours—at least eight hours every night, if not more, combined with afternoon naps on the weekends—continued well into my twenties, thirties, and even early forties. I did this out of habit because getting "enough sleep" had been drilled into my mind as an important part of healthy living. Whenever I felt tired, I assumed it was because I hadn't gotten a good enough sleep the night before. So, I'd try to sleep even *more* to make up for it.

A little while ago, something clicked for me: I've been chronically tired for most of my life.

This clicked for me when I *stopped* feeling chronically tired around two years ago—when I was forced to work two jobs, seven days per week, to restore my finances. One of my jobs was working with the morning crew for a local drug store chain. My weekend shifts ran from 5 AM to 9 AM. My weekday shifts, for my regular full-time job, started at 7:30 AM downtown which meant I had to leave my house by at least 7 AM for the commute.

I remember the first time my alarm went off at 4 AM for that first morning crew shift. I was shocked by it and thought, "I'm *never* going to be able to do this." But, out of necessity, I did it. I got used to it. And, by the time my shifts were over, I had tons of energy and the whole day ahead of me to write my books.

About a year ago, I decided to set my alarm for 4 AM every single day of the week. I do my best writing first thing in the morning, so I decided to put *me* first every single day and write for two hours before getting into the shower to get ready for work. I continue to write in the evenings whenever I can, too.

I've gotten my sleep down to between six and seven hours every night, and I've completely cut out afternoon naps. I have *way* more energy for doing it. I'm a far more productive individual because of this change in my sleeping habits. I thank God for this "accidental" discovery!

Recommended Resources on Sleep Habits

Get More Hours In Your Day: http://www.keypersonofinfluence.com/get-more-hours-in-your-day/ "Having looked at successful people like Sir Richard Branson, I found that many are members of the elite 5am Club who begin their day at 5 in the morning."

Is sleeplessness REALLY the key to Donald's success? Researchers are baffled after Trump's doctor praised the president's four-hour sleep cycle: https://www.dailymail.co.uk/health/article-5284457/Donald-Trump-sleeps-four-hours-night-wise.html "'How does somebody that's sleeping 12 and 14 hours a day compete with someone that's sleeping three or four?' Trump said in 2009."

I Decided to Sleep for 4 Hours a Day, See What Happened: https://www.youtube.com/watch?v=lbFzL-0pEeU "If your life is like one big to-do list that you just can't seem to keep up with, then polyphasic sleep is probably for you. All jokes aside, I definitely became more productive, and I have a lot of spare time that allows me to do everything I want and even more."

IT'S TIME TO MAKE *YOUR* DREAM COME TRUE

The beauty of being a writer in this digital age is that writing *is* selling in the online world. It's as though the Internet was built just for us writers, isn't it? We are precious commodities to online marketers and other business people who wish to hire copywriters and ghostwriters to help them publish blog posts and books. Best of all, we can write and publish our own blog posts and books—and *finally* earn a decent living doing what we love to do. It's possible!

Your dream may resemble mine in some ways, or you may be inspired to follow an entirely different path than me. My best advice is to follow your own intuition and have faith in your ability to achieve your heart's desire. I hope the tools and guidance provided throughout this book series is most useful to you along your journey; and I hope you'll share your success story with my blog subscribers in a guest post some day. I welcome that.

Whenever you come across obstacles that test your faith along the way, please read this book again. Use it to restore your faith by reading the stories of all these people who succeeded against incredible odds. They're just like you. You're just like them. Jim Carrey said it best when he said this:

> "Your imagination is always manufacturing scenarios, both good and bad. And the ego tries to keep you trapped in the multiplex of the mind. Our eyes are not only viewers; they're also projectors that are running a second story over the picture that we see in front of us all the time. Fear is writing that script, and the working title is 'I'll

Never Be Enough.' ... No matter what you gain, ego will not let you rest. It will tell you that you cannot stop until you've left an indelible mark on the earth, until you've achieved immortality. How tricky is this ego that it would tempt us with the promise of something we already possess? Relax, and dream up a good life."
~Jim Carrey, 2014 Maharishi University of Management Commencement Address

In other words, there's nothing at all to fear. There's never any reason to procrastinate. Write your book. Publish it. Sell it. Enjoy the ride! I hope this creates untold wealth for you.

BIBLIOGRAPHY

Hill, N. (1937). *Think and Grow Rich.* United States of America: Meriden, Conn. | Ralston Society.

McGregor, J. (2017, May 25). *Amazon Pays $450,000 A Year To This Self-Published Writer*. Retrieved from Forbes: https://www.forbes.com/sites/jaymcgregor/2015/04/17/mark-dawson-made-750000-from-self-published-amazon-books/#2779f9fc6b5b

Pilkington, E. (2012, January 12). *Amanda Hocking, the writer who made millions by self-publishing online.* Retrieved from The Guardian: https://www.theguardian.com/books/2012/jan/12/amanda-hocking-self-publishing

Proctor, B. (2017, September 22). Bob Proctor on How to Visualize, Think and Grow Rich & Reading | Matei Catalin YouTube video: https://www.youtube.com/watch?v=ZsrFT5WPyb w. (M. Catalin, Interviewer)

Schruers, F. (1995, July 13). *Jim Carrey: Bare Facts and Shocking Revelations*. Retrieved from Rolling Stone: https://www.rollingstone.com/culture/culture-news/jim-carrey-bare-facts-and-shocking-revelations-181569/

Smith, W. (n.d.). The Mindset of High Achievers | MulliganBrothers YouTube video: https://www.youtube.com/watch?v=LhV6RItLs84&t=33s. (Unknown, Interviewer)

Smith2, W. (n.d.). Will Smith - Focus and Determination | Xeniafoon1988 YouTube video:

https://www.youtube.com/watch?v=rRE_o7YWwfs
. (Unknown, Interviewer)

Wattles, W. D. (1910). *The Science of Getting Rich.* New
York: Elizabeth Towne Publishing New York.

Winfrey, O. (n.d.). Master Class with Oprah Winfrey,
Exclusive Interview | LUX4RT YouTube video:
https://www.youtube.com/watch?v=9vs0zAHfl0M.
(Unknown, Interviewer)

INDEX

ABOUT THE AUTHOR

So many people are publishing books of all kinds nowadays, and they need guidance regarding best practices with everything from writing to publishing to selling those books. I've made it my life's mission to help others navigate this mysterious business littered with acronyms and peculiar old-fashioned practices.

As a bestselling author and TESOL-certified sales coach for authors with 25 years' experience in the North American English book publishing industry (in both the traditional and contemporary markets), I can show you how to write, publish, and sell your book(s) using all the effective traditional and online tricks of the trade. Add my substantial advertising sales and marketing background into the mix, and you have a serious mentor in front of you who can help you achieve commercial success as an author.

If your goal is to produce a professional quality book that you can sell commercially, the team at Polished Publishing Group (PPG) can help. We teach authors how to write a book, how to publish a book, how to sell a book. Professional project management services are also available.

Visit my company website here:
https://polishedpublishinggroup.com/

Visit my blog here:
https://blog.polishedpublishinggroup.com/